Vanished Pursuit
Into A Remembered Future

Douglas Blazek

EDITION
MUTA

Grateful acknowledgment is offered to the editors of the following journals, in which these poems first appeared in earlier versions: *Aldebaran Review, Arion's Dolphin, Beloit Poetry Journal, Brown Sweater, Connections, Consumption, Corduroy, Delirium, Dragonfly, Eureka Review, Floating Island, Hearse, The Hiram Poetry Review, Iconolatre, Laughing Bear, Monument, Oink, Open Places, Poetry Now, Quercus, Some, South Florida Review, Suenos, Third Rail, Vagabond, Wormwood Review*

News of a Useless Thing was first published as a chapbook by Prismatic Navigator Press, 2009

Published by Edition Muta
www.editionmuta.com

FIRST EDITION

Paperback   MUTA 07   ISBN 978-0-9850044-8-4
Special edition   MUTA 07   X

For My Father –
Having given me all I needed
to love by the words you gave.

And for Rachel –
Who gives more words.

Contents

The Visit

I climb the stairs to a room
where I've never been. Enter
the same door never entered.

From a drawer never opened
I take a living sheet of oblivion
and place it on the table. Pour
my name to the missing middle
letting it spread to every edge
darkening the sheet to evening.

From a recess never traced
I withdraw an unaddressed
envelope and animistic ink.
Then a pen to shaman
my charlatans into antlers.

All the shoes never worn
are scuffed within a closet.
A slum of gloves, clutching
stubborn fait accompli,
await what has come.

Through the floor a ladder
ascends to extend my visit.
I slip my hands into my gloves,
my feet into my shoes
and step upon a rung.

The Complexity of a Thing I Do Obsessively

I lock myself in an orthodox
box. Tuck and overlap
a flux of flaps.
Thoughts extrapolate thoughts.
Extract optics
that observe my box.

It's like living in the ticket
booth to a movie theater
selling tickets to imposters
all bothering to be me.

With deja vu in the viewing seats,
screened information
sifts the future
spoken by ghostly solipsists
in linguistic insurrection.

The movie obliges a man
to climb a one-rung ladder:
thesaurus of his thesis
moving exegesis
to exercise its speed.

I unlock the box
but am kept in custody of the script.
To survive I must revise
the agony of the protagonist.

Despite an ending
the script remains unfinished.
The imposition of its input
situates a spot
where unbidden possibility
impossibly steps out.

Inner Marathons

A struggling puppet,
diving deepsea skin,
entangles his strings
deep in another puppet.

Within a sea of scissors
he retrieves but mirrors,
and there, unangled,
confronts his entangler.

Sorting disorder's
discordant coordinates
he confirms their terms'
co-terminus control:
indigenous invisible
fingers indivisible
to the things they pull.

Not wanting to struggle
or be a knot, but mostly
to not be a puppet
or dive, he runs to derive
an end to his lateral
fall composing a lapping
to surpass the mobius
path of puppetry.

Snipping unfinish lines
with scissor-steps
is simply aquatics slipping
within its simulacral sea
seeing through seeing's
edgeless center
ever verging to vertex
as depth reversed.

The Hole: An Autobiography

A man transcends
by expanding into a hole
a hole

the man proclaims
made by lightning
each moment his mind expands.

Parts of his parts
mirror particles
miming mirrors.
Sites that dilate
bind the allure
his eyes obscure.

Suffering while stuck
in utterance, the man
calls his voice's bluff,
causal without a cause,
leaving without absence
but coming back as its past's
pre-post advance.

Inadvertently, the hole
converts nothing it knows
to the whole of its knowing.
The man keeps circling
a word's self-return
turning its certainty
through its wordless center
like a fuse sending the universe
through lightning.

A Tour of Easy Torture

A day of joyrays—
skies raised
beyond any gauge of mind.
A day of torn laundry's
ragged wrens cleansed
and mended by their raddled
praise of morning.

Nailed nuptials of a picket
motion picture smile
their energetic idleness
at fidelity's affections.

Today my private terminus
flies its public kite
verved toward vertical
peril to defy
its spiral tether
as wind for higher pleasure

unties its springy weather
observing my evolving
tour of easy torture—
awareness with no awarer
dismentaled by its mentor
edging to its edge
but centered in its center.

Street Song in October

Sidetracked
on my way to eternity
by storefront Baptist baritones,
clustered gusty swarmflies
lusting a handful of god's sweetdung...

and chrome-preened pickups
prowling asphalt, scratching
a randy screech, burning rowdy sperm...

and a crimson spree of leaves,
chinese crinkled kites
dipping and diving
in sportcrash and glorywheel...

and the women, Sunday women,
highheeled and hairpyred,
robed in flirtdom fur,
queenish twilight tigers
keening behind each eye...

And as this dress rehearsal
choreographs its metamorphosis
deeper into October,
my fastest procrastinating feet
advance one step to another
to another that is dance:

rapidity intricately exiting
inhabiting ignition's
instant absence.

This Day is Immortal

This day, its populist
outspoken stunt men
tumbling my brain
tripping their flippant
tricks of trade out
imprisoned incipience
into ambitious extravagance
cryptically ubiquitous.

This day, a turbulence
blurred in alembic remembrance.
Emotionally colossal
fossil-fleshings awakening
sensations's ancient potential.

This day, eased
as a spy through my eye's
belief that its identity
is identical to sight
hiding in vision's
pervasive invasion.

Each day! Husked rays
caressing me with naked newness,
crushing me brazenly into the grave
immortality calls radiance!

This Common Day on the Vine

I reveal. I conceal.
Found in appearance
hidden in what's found.
Imprisoned in this freedom,
my terminal circularity,
its periphery's antithesis,
prods oroboric rara avis
to anti-doubted rapprochement.

Just words vs. words.
Rhapsodic despots
forging erotic forays.
Just a way to kiss.

Just cunning linguistics
skirting my covetous tongue.
Just words in estrus
vexing my cerebral musk.

Imaxed hag-sex resurrecting
my erection forgetting
I'm a stapled paper man
mazed in a fabled magazine.

Forgetting I am fleshed to the vine
fed by one great flame
MapQuesting the matrix
that grapens my life to wine.

This common day is libidinous,
sinuous with nirvanic
venom— premonitious
vibrations advancing
my chancing viper-charmer's
ambitious nonchalance.

Operatic Mirage

Yes, I am the city's
promiscuous interdiction
exalting in contexturous
asphalt and brick!

Cracks in a sidewalk,
nexus of flux,
concupiscence quaking
love to a fault.

Endogenous astrology,
lavishly lolling
in erogenous qualia
cosmically facading
its operatic mirage.

Versions of emergence,
vertex to vista,
impass through glass
richly expelling
fascistic irrelevance.

A hat, cold-crushed
by collaborative traffic,
abandons its head
to rafter my attic:

a hazardly synaptic
aspirant hatch
incepted in hex
ordinary and ornate
ancient as chanting
enchanted as chance.

A Cellular Song

Saturn Avenue, Jupiter Lane,
Boulevard of Mars...
a city mirrored in its Mercury...

A spider edges out its web
having stitched the universe
round its turning point yearning
for a little planet to molest.

Through a window, the aura
of the moon is as nude
as me in my tub. Below
its lumen's hovering rapport,
I cajole l'amour to lower.
To hug and scrub as soap.

I bathe today
in a version of birthwater
mulling a lullaby
into motherly words
offering their service
as a way to their source.

Churning down the drain,
a liquid skip of surplus
cells burnish the rings of Saturn,
rub the rust off Mars

invigorate the charm of reticular
atoms, their quantum tang
a fresh circumscription
stretching great distance
round inches of flesh.

Moment

Moon frost
on the washroom
window.
Death mask
off its distance
to scrim the edge
of my skinning stare
shared afar
akin my disappearing
hands glistening
dark off each other.
Water lost in water.
Time washing time.
A moment
sowing its complexion
to departure.
Progression growing
traceless patterns
layered-on.
Awareness feathered-in.
Sun within sun
purging
more tons of hydrogen.

An old December rests on window's
infancy. Snow without scold.
Exposure quoting breath's quotidian blur.
Whiteness future-frozen, re-writing its use.
Once a solemn, private pallor
oversitting where everything sat
outwaiting the incoming fancy
that never advanced.
Now it stretches adjacency
to replace names of anonymity.
Now any jaunt is chancy
as I movingly sit at my inescapable table
attending the distance of present things,
skin replacing skin, stained
reach of mind bleached into an unplanned
aim. An empty bowl and a blank
spoon each cradling the other's consecration.

To Finish What I Cannot Start

When it's done I can do it.
Dance as accomplished accident.
A slip on wet thought.

Dwarves sleep in mountain wit.
Some slip downstream and jam-up.
When enough jam there are giants.

Difference is untimed synchronics.
Separate planets together
attracting the other's wobble.

It is done when I do not do it.
Frost trusts its finished attraction.
With diligence I trace the pattern.

Nature Study

I focus both faucets
to frolic their flow
flushing suds
from stubble once humble
now crowish grown
raucous to my face.

Splash is havoc
having shattered control.
Foam around oath:
an epiphany lifting
loud above lips.
Clouds after cholic
raining my rivered name.

Nature, in its contours,
mirrors the curves
my visceral benediction
akins under skin—
diverging : converging.
Forking in fulcrum.
Connective in genuflect.

Autumn's tumbledown intoxication
slows its slowest sipped violas
passing loss to its last quartet.

Apple branches tap the air's
anarchic scaffolding
rivet-rattling a reticular bridge.

All vagabond wovenness
confides its tattle's open habitat
to a microphone's silent sky.

A gardener's proverbs underground
arrange their gambit anagrams
verging out their verdant mounds.

A colossal terminus in us
adopts its middle's ousted ends
taking turns outtaking loss.

Rinsing ether
through their atoms,
the leaves now
are almost sky-skin.
Traveling past
the edge of attachment,
each rendering
leaves its reading
for another.
Mystery, this very
morning, is having tea
with a tourist.
So what if autumn
scalesdown separation
that once kept
wind from mind
yet kept mind porus?
Whatever wavering
there is, hasn't
air all fitted
together?

Autumn By Winter's End

Some sort of emotional
tree just
opened all its color
so spectrum's expression
can re-set precedent.
So a beholder's awareness
can reword misnomers
in a world's current reign.
So autumn
can evoke post-knowing
as the telescope's
spoken lens
refrained in a realm
free of extension's
meaning.
Agedly complex,
yet ever in the earth's
wrong place, the tree
places its shaman
in a cloud's mouth.
What came as time
rains again its augury
gnawing the air's
raw transparence
preparing a fahrenheit
ark of ice.

Pocket Map in the Apple

Our store-bought oracle planted
like a dazzling ornament
out back in that patch
of grandiosity is growing
a grotesque palace, allegorical
with undermall and a roof
that could crush the earth.
Eventually, the documentary
we spend our epoch devising
becomes a proxy paradise.
And from this paradise
an apple tree with a pocket
map inside each apple
branches through our narration
where the same clouds
rain every day and the darkest
lightning above the target
of our head keeps splitting
open the apple path
to extrude our reddening errancy
like a worm savior.

Wind Within Against Its Storm

Rowdy wind.
Leaves dodging
their collide with time
down to their final
fatal harmony—
and the angling rain applauds
raw the apples
clanging on the trees,
seeds concordantly
ringing in their cores—
and the cores agree: everything
engaged will ring and clang
within against its storm
amassing emphatic static
ripening snaps of light.
And, if this sound is torment,
it is song. Earth proven
not wrong but autumn.
Momentum from its force
a course for counterforce.
Thus ferment for the advancing worm
tastes ancestrally sweet.
The eons it eats are the poorest
aftermath to the wealth of apples.
So, in all this phosphorescent
sweat, what work is left
for the flash of death?

Suspending the years
so airy only a bird's
memory of aerodynamics resembles it.
Silence quivery without flight.
Travel inherent in self-aware vigor.
Quest is the quarry
that swallows the hours
digesting a word about to be written
something coercively uncertain
urgently discursive
enough to spur itself through its own source—
an alarm clock that starts the shot
that penetrates the brain
sleeping with all its presets
screwing all the news.
Who is awake?

Everything By a Thousand Names

In a thousand current years
our compost flesh
will have nurtured a forest,
possessor of our effort
to survive our effect—
green carrion marrying
a thousand names to come.

Completion is what part of sequence?
Which snipped piece sharpens
its sleuth to coup sum with scissors?

An aphasic catastrophe agilely
matures gradually in nature
greater than any archaic mansion
crumbling to command the land.

Owning the eye is owning
the submission of what is pictured
to inhabit as master
the coup de grace predator of time.

A Funny Way to Be Serious

Humor is useless
unless unruly true— unless
wildly designing the size
of its lion to live in you.

Roar is the rigor
an ocean self-controls
owning the way a woman is loved
the love she lets go.

Incessance is the motion
it sows emerging
explosion into the urge
incontinence holds.

Unwedded knowledge
spreads to marriage
message-stepping up the stem
beheading what pretends the brain.

Watch your eyes blossom
the impossible iris. Watch
vision solicit its novice
flourish to nourish flow.

Maintenance the Wang Wei Way

Hell, my soul's okay!
Like a tree on fire:
brighter the flame
deeper its roots reach for water.
And if suffering is snuffed
after flashes of death,
my soul ransacks the dark
to ignite again what condemns
it to an arsonist's life.
Afar there is more.
My soul's an abjure-janitor.
It burns trash to heat its art.
And soon an ember's
dharmic connoisseur
crackles ash's greenest startle.

Li Po's Flow

The tyranny of desperately
clutched truth–
how its audibles
hawk the cloying
lawlessness
of its power-gaudy
cause. How it garbles
its assault to an upstart
corpse of culture.

Li Po's river
stocked with poems
flows beyond
rock or wrong.
Ink's portal course,
prolonged
by incorporeal pen,
sinks to turn
what returns to sink
creeling its unleakable
water wheel.

Loud with thirst
we unfist
a drinkable search
unfurling words
air converts
quietly sprinkling
the universe.

Tu Fu: Master Traveler

He keeps stepping into holes.
Holes the size of Om.
Holes not known to the mind
stigmatic round its axis
compacting its existence
into piles of reactive pits.
His foot widens absence
just a crack to fit
the once of omnipotence
actual in an unyet place
while every race runs past
asking why he breaks
with what the world expects.

Lilacs

A glass of cut lilacs.

Just blouseless flowers.
Sepal cells
revealing
the enormous cathedral
our amnesia
adores.

An initient
thing
persistently
springing
incipient
if to *is.*

An alchemist,
fluting
test tube beauty
from within its bloom,
fits to future's
growing mouthpiece
a glass-blown
breath
pre-musically
used,
shatter-fused.

Lavender, traited
for another nature,
endeavors its trust
up the adaptive ladder
leaving us
a love to climb
our life for.

Flowering Echoes

Trellised chisels
strike design
arcing trysted sparks
behind the eyes'
clandestine scarlet.

Love's pyromania
remaining prior
emblazons fragrance
from heart's synapse
perhapsing brain's bouquet.

A spade in topsoil,
toiling solid vacancy,
aches in the heat
of unexposed seed.

Yards and yards, sychronically
sown, shared with a farther field.

A gust of time suggests
the guest of distance
has come and stopped
and left but left within
each manifest thing
shuffled wind's
pranic compass.

Echoes, flowering
directions for eons
to follow, request
their ions to model
for human bucolics
a binding embodied
diffused in finding.

The Concert Resumes

A fresh sun stretches
its arms, nods to the stars,

maestro-taps earthen
musicians strewn

in botanic drowse,
and the day begins:

a cellular melody rushes
its spell out of mulch

troping its notes
to open their total

tender vibrato, their vast
resurgent verve

elastically scattered
yet wholly gathered

in speculate aspects
of lavish multiplicity

echoically quoting
their inner ovation,

pervasive versions
praising an even larger

playing, a perished recurrence
coaxing a forcefield's

accord: entropy flexing
its next unexpected score.

The passage I hum
segues assertion to another
assertion entraining my tongue's
obversification
coercing refrain to change.

Song's surfaced encumbrance,
once sub-atomic ruckus,
tucks into the structure of Brahms:
remembrance struggling
its menace to portend
corpuscular alms.
Simultaneity of realities
sorted and played
to liberate the spiritual
little more than literal
from forebrained cliche.

Ranged but estranged,
morphemes, extremed,
re-hearting hearing's
annealing pain, sweeten
a spree of self-rape—
raptured abstraction's
systolic splay
of neologic notes.

And Brahms, dear
Brahms, this morning
keeps scouting devoutly
the score's self-trust.
Grace of apex
roughly fussing
out a vacuum flux.

Impromptus in Parts

Glassy grass
this icy day—
ideal keys
my eye's
glazier needs
to frame
a playable inquiry.

Note-by-note
I try to write
what the ice
book wrote
enticed by crystal
ink's
cryptic source
scored
to flow
frozen torque
out instrument.

Solos, totaled
in constellations,
little by little
evolve the whole—
ellipsised
windows on a trillion
grand pianos—
clairvoyant foreplay
teasing
my fingers
to see.

Etude of So-What

It must get taught
how the oldest
polychromals
encode an apple's
core with crimson
sorcery to correlate
space-rapport
with aftertaste.
Or how a flute
in doubt's debut
circulating music's
truthless truth
plays the etudes'
greatest route.
No where to go.
Nothing to do.
Clockwise or not.
Was or was knot
tying what's sought
to the naught of so-what.

The Melody of a Marble

Still
the alluvium
of a trillion tuned universe
delighting discursively
in aleatory play.
Turnstiled detritus
splurging its spin
merging what's fiddled
from cosmic string.
Mars in a marble
enthroned in routine
droning roulette.
Catalyst of genesis
ricocheting its genius
for genetic effect.
Melody a chaos
connecting its bets
remaking its notes
from payoff mistakes.
Music's reason
chances cohesion
reasonably secret
in the playing of it.

Orange Dreams

Just a whiff of astronomic
apparition
and we're after it
grafting space's
thin narration
to body's gravity
gone orange.
What fire isn't virgin
perished
in desire's plunge?
What self-burn
isn't whirlwind
urged by orange?
Sealed in its dream's
incompletion, the world
births its womb.
Every endeavor tethers
metastic catastrophe
to its absolution
in origin's skin.
Our volatile mind,
exhausting the spoils
of its forging,
engorges
the author of orange.

Orange
and I
are edible, vulnerable
to an indelible hunger.
Back and forth
across a spacious platter
we converse
chewing
civilities into quiddity's
previous
peptic perception,
mulling introspectively
the meanings
we continuously
eat:
seed, rind, pulp
speech-to-bowels
flushbowl-
to-cesspool
creek-to-river-
to-sunrise-sea
surprised
as origin
devouring again
its own recognition.

Matter Born to Matter Again

Scissors, in metaphysical siesta,
awaken to snip particles from wave
so all the fables in waiting
can shuffle their days on stage.

Inexplicable tricksters conflict
in indeterminate air. Watchers
watch what appears to occur.
To weather a watching everywhere.

What foretells of ruin is ruin's
reform construed in the rules
returnings use coming
from ruined forthcomings.

But the play of counterplay
compounds the way play unbounds
so transactions can transcend
their contractual happenings.

So aspect's habits can expose
their pose masquerading
as moments freshly cast
by longing elapsed prolonged.

All cards, in a system of separation,
discard their schism, re-shuffle
their agreement's unerring scheme:
matter born to matter again.

Youth Executed

Libidinous little chisels
sculpt the athletic mannequin
trained in manly momentum
inaugurating the family album.

Clutched in a fist of solstice,
a crystalline avalanche
carbonized its acrobats.
Starlings scratch their charcoal
screech across the watchword sky.
Creeks outcrawl their frozen cracks
to gush a trap of underpath.

Disagreeable necessity
leads to reflex–
paycheck's ancestral wreckage
aggressively presaged.

Years erode. The family
album now is closed,
a yellowed soured eros.
Enthusiasm for youth's
adrenaline has morosed
to deaf forensics.
Elects to execute the truth.

Slumped in the coldest snow,
shot by loaded hopes,
blood pours its oldest man
down a granite blossom
into the grayest storm
eroding granite stone.

Metabolism

At work, I take the breakage
of my thought's watch
and toss it
to the blast furnace—
watch it blacken
to ash. Vanish to gas.

Time into time
time through time
time out of time
every time
every I
I into I
I through I
I out of I.

Vast actuals
at one
moment, suddenness
at another.

Nothing to advance
or advance to—
scrutiny consuming energy
as it consumes me.

My Art is the Art of Tensions

As if love were steel
by yards and years,
my effort curls to a torque
of marriage. Soon
a little spring pinks up
cringing its specifics,
crying to be synchronized.
Then, unexpectedly, another spring
complexes the family!
From wherever there is air
offsprings of these springs spring:
needs, keen and teasing—
so with my knees and toes
wrists and elbows
nose and chin
I begin my incessant
flexing and bending
for a blended, balanced
ballet, a playful display
of anatomical agony.
My art is the art
of tensions. Tripwire
itches defiantly tuned
to musical dissonance—
crucial antithesis
almost congruence.
Ever a dance
pledged in misstep.
Exacting resistence
practicing yes
reflexed in legs.

Marriage

Marriage was more a crater
than a trunk.

Down it they dumped
a sullen sofa, disdainful rugs,
anxious blankets, a snappy toaster,
ravaged pots of cooked disaster, a bleak tv,
books that reeked of words deceased.

They dumped and dumped
mounding a hole above the ground.

They fought the wounds
of the other's other.
Power thrust to puncture power.
To crust pus across the crater.

They fought the wind's
syringe of air.
Fought for saviors'
lipsynced stars
binging kisses
on puckered pain.
They starved to death
from death's saliva injected
live.

Attack was the blackest
passion backing
in and out
the hole that gags
what leaves
and goes back in.

Night Like a Crater Upsidedown

A crater upsidedown, out
of and pulled over
itself, night

sites its hermetic
dialectics of light.
Ubiquitous self-witnessed
portals transfixed:

perforations forfeiting
their expected directions:
exit

thick as an endless door.

Grief Deeper Into Grief

Darkness burnished into night.
Grief's incubation.
Pain's purpose as preparation.

Intensity pre-dimensionally
sensing a bruised
lumination. Tincture's
immutable substance
flooding itself. Waves
attempting to contain
the continent they touched.

Obsession's neuronal scold
too stulted but to control in cluster.
But to regress its lingual
predator to the hiss of a spiritualist.

Ambitious intuition
keeps fishing its whip
flipping residual
pity out its cataclysmic pit.

A grave keeps nailing
deeper its nil. Friction
gestating its raid. Speck
of iron nictitating the brain.

A spark that shocks its light.
All fire one flame
enduring sheen beneath the skin.
An explosion's total
happening
just before it opens.

Creation Against Chronology

I know god is not
pleasant.
That suffering
is stubborn.
Subterranean without bloom.
That consolation means
the cost of change
is dunned hourly
but is dumb.
I have not remembered
or forgotten
how the Big Bang
is known
by my cells,
its echoic totality
lent in increments
as steps to intelligence–
crenelations racing
creation against chronology
borrowing in absentia
what summation contains.
Life and death
just right and left.
In thought,
this is nice.
In actuality,
it is not.

My runaway awareness
keeps running stop signs
non-stop.
My inner brakes
lapse
their reluctance
to rush
into crash.

Dissonant Innocence

I stroll with chips and coke
from the squeeze-in soda shop
over to where artists from the Institute
sprawl and sketch
what air reveals of its barrenness.
I bend to body-mat the grass
under a posthumous god and goddess
embraced in thunderous bronze,
their stolen purpose opposing
its unchosen pose.
A pose now juxtaposed
to the sweaty aroma of the soul's algorithm
apt and unexpected
pre-etched on every pad, pre-scratched
on the slated brain, working
its dissonant innocence
up stratas into strokes
heroic aesthetic etiquette
texturing-in the rabble
of breasts and testicles

A locus of occasions dislocates
its aim to a scattered
center entered
to re-gather something greater
grown as focus
exploded to foliage.

A displacement of place
passes its phrasing
onto an oncoming page
opening its topos
to roads out its matrix
protracting the asking
that proposes a maze.

A word is a way
through its wayward effect,
an aperture's praise
appraising emergence
branching further
its self-atlasing path—
and just think—
Omar Khayyam
keeps urging up apples
somewhere in Persia.

Stepping into the Step Stepping Still

Strewn with speech debris
the street I sweep
determines the ground of indeterminacy.

Polarities larynxed from paradoxed ink
face the facets
integral opposites traverse to connect.

To travel afar referred to as here.

Yet further.

To where chance
directs indirection of steps
making chance by intent
step after step

a passage reflecting
what saying obstructs
stalled in its utterance

still as its target.

Thief of the Last Dimension

As a thief I keep
stealing what my spy
needs to be
to rival its limits
layered of light.

To kiss the laminate
my lips
peel to see.

I steal a wardrobe's
storehouse of borders:
mirrors meshing my skin
incesting reflections
undressing within.
Edges complexing
the task of regression
stretching its end
to outer dimension.

I see where here is elsewhere,
where elsewhere
is other
wearing my face
in layered disguise
as a spy in a spy.
The last dimension is nothing
but mask.
Trapdoored and skylighted.

Parsec After Genesis

Accosting not just the costume
but the style it occults,
a pulse's articulation
coaxes striations to untie
their hostage of heart—
to wear impartial nirvana
now artless as air.

Leaping through language,
Columbus on springs
far-flinging misfeasance
ripping planks from the ship
fleecing the sails bleating
serration's sky-bled sheep.

An ocean's hydraulics
pliers gold ingots
so shipwrecks can purchase
rich sips of dawn.

Discovery has no custom.
Just love for what comes.
Just vastness to love.
No dub from the past.

Parsec after genesis
quarkly dispersed into aspects
of apex crushed into earth
so vortex so vowed
as the prow of cosmos
can plow its proof
through syntactic clues
pixel-riveted, mouth-mixed.

Vanishment Subsisting in Its Ventriloquy

I carve words to caress
the dimensionless cradle
of a cosmic sarcophagus.
Tomb figures finessed
by its cognizant wattage.

Something hurries past.
I stick out my foot.
Trip it to pivot, not plummet.
To fit my interior summit.
Just strings of wind
puppeting a circling up.

Finis loves the story of forever.
Loves the notes between polkas.
Evening disrobing motioning to morning.
A chance to dance.
Steps to re-set precedence.

Watch my thought
self-slice its thinking—
truthified lightning
through butchersky skin—
fluttering's quintessence
soliciting its infinite
laminate of chrysalis.

Something seeks in me
the means to be free of what it seeks.
To last in a lasting dispersed.
Vanishment subsisting in its ventriloquy
inextricably stitching
ether's pictures to speech.

Within the Within

The road coaxes at the door:
follow me, it says,
stretch your reach's feedback
to test its task.
But I cannot leave.
I am too much the forest in a tree.

Road, your call is stalled
in each word's installment.
Batons in a marathon
passing on their run-on re-run
to score what's moored
in past rewards.

I am coming, but not budging.
Your lifeline is my spine
circulating the uncertainty
of my inner terrain
displacing unaimed distractions
with what attracts my aim.

My cramped writing knuckle
crimps the travel
the actual unravels.
Planetary strands
in phantom conflation
reconfigured as paths
for synaptic advancement.

A Rock in the House

A pound of mountain
propping open the door.
Enormity hobbled.
A priori no more.
Consolation out foraging
what greater formation
is for.

All local unfolding
vastly non-local.
A massless cul-de-sac
overlapping subtraction
adding itself
to a sum self-solved:
a given untaken,
part of creation,
equivocal fraction
of original riddle
fit to the middle of the middle.

Algorithmic indeterminates.
Bits to characteristics.
Amalgamate of contested time.
Holographic exits. Dust,
a smaller us, edge-fixed,
holy contexted.

Mineralflesh awareness,
as instants in extremis
shared by the universe,
advances past
ubiquitous specifics
taking the planet
with it.

For Those Who Love

Here in the kitchen
reciprocity prepares
a recipe for breath.

Culinary elements
suffered by cosmos
reserved for the mouth:

spoons of theology
knives of psychology
forks of physics

obtusive soup
critiqued meat
trick-slit fruit.

In the table's grain,
laws swallow stains
of interpolated talk.

Kitchen meridians, kinnery
feast, vows of agreement
a novice attentively takes.

Pertinence

Stove pot odor, solar
fire socialized
round the kitchen table.
Talk's taste displacing
toast. Molecules in a tea
bowl moved by a momumental
scholar. Connections
odder than orange.
Parenthetical utterance
husked like quantum corn.
Insomnia encrypted in a mystical nap
enjoins us with zest.
Raw conflictual physics
renewed in the nuance of tongues
muscle-lifting pertinence–
everything's participation makes
awake what fits.

Breakfast in Heaven

A bell is ringing—
a sweet faint far-away bell:
breakfast in heaven.

Morning reclines on warm concrete.
Green climbs into its grassest ether.
Bees knit the air's invisible lattice.
A cat peeks catless at a sleeping cat.

This is not the world but a painting
living its private life off canvas.

The canvas exists in a museum.
You can go see it.
You can sit on the bench
and content yourself
inventing a dream of reasons
unusable but true.

An artist will enter.
He will hand you his paints and a brush.
Of course, you paint the bell.

What There Is to Eat

I eat astonishment:
snatching its provisional passing
indirectly in all directions.
A synapse's perhaps, eye latched.

I eat incomprehension:
questions exponentially suffering
solipsistically their echoic omens.
Options too complexly over-opted to open.

I eat momentum:
omens, forcefeeding their forcefield
dream, bring to fore a farther motion:
power forged to forge more power.

This is my mission:
to eat vicious to posthumous.
Loss revised if viable in visceral.
Systems invisible in systems.

Hunger Dream

I dream I am a slice of rye
in a delicatessen, a lover
of seed seasoning ham.

Urging the success of pleasure,
splurging a careless mess of mustard,
I molest the incestuous flavors,

suck a lucky wreck of kraut
down the dice cup of my mouth
gambling for highrise surprise.

In the morning I eat oatmeal
and yogurt and curse vengeance
upon my slum of spoon.

Victims of Inattention

Back-to-back, unlanguaged
with cadence clacking in the waves
trying to interrogate the sea,
immediacies knead their speed's
wavering changes
changing what they ever see.
Sun's breathing to win its breath.
Life hissed in the living of it.
Each story untold in the telling.
Unwritten in the weeping.
Victims of inattention
drift in no intent
attempting the ever present:
a ship, visceral,
with its cargo
waterlit all around it.

Drowned in the Holy Disowned

Rains chained to unconstrained reins
aimed by mono-reign's chain of command
commonly claimed by common man.

Cake and cream passed around.
Celebration tastes of deep abyss.
Christfish trawled like christless mist.

Raining where the wettest world
dreams to drain, mass panic
sucks manic/womanic

down to where wealth
reveals what riches conceal
drowned in the holy disowned.

Flux and Reflux

Analogues of order
enter to alter
oar forms in water—
tensions attained
by netherous tether.

Restless crenelations
etch their edges'
implications
fissuring sensations
to infinite regress.

Incessant discursiveness
further unfurls
incipient diversiveness
meshing insurgents
with plural implexity.

Flux and reflux
construct, with mystery's
memory, energy's ingenuity,
the ineluctable synergy
of evening's ruin

suffused to morning's
auric coordinates
sorting ruckused
recombinant rays
untamed, extempored.

The Classic Look of Eternity

Sand disperses
its restless awareness
stirring particularity
into clarity's blur.

Rushing
through its watery
snare the oceanal roar
emancipates
contour.

Sea-rocks
gleaming a skidding glass
reflect spent flecks
of recklessness.

Wind balks
its swift slapped
gusts of stuttered
indulgence.

An immoveable sky
falls infused
with all it sees
bleeding cobalt
into gravity.

Suddenly
momentum's effects
ransack their quest
attracting pandemonium's
impact intact.

Here, where quiddity
tests its quintessence,
I hear the raconteur
of Sunday bliss:
a gull teasing loose
a strand of limbic mist
lingering on the edge
of light's shed lingerie

on the edge
where the sea
seamlessly
caresses
its erotic chaos
kissing persistence
out fear of cessation.

Toward my car
I crash against
crosspurpose:
rain tacking rain
hatching the original
directions of wind.

A bulletin
from physics
expresses
the news:

immutable atoms
natural datum
diffuse and infusible
shuffle their one
hit-and-run.

I

Along the shore the ocean
adores no picture, rushes
its roar toward the backwash,
over starfresh stillness of sand,
to spill its passage of vastness.

Versions pressed in succession
display inertia's dispersion,
compose option's composite,
displacing abstract splash
with after-image supplication.

Brine-marled partial designs
depict, in cryptic equivalents,
the critical force an infinite intent
releases in waves, in relentless
kinetics for a photogenic grave.

II

Languorous, then intense,
the ocean churns, pounds,
bellows the same sound
we try to say naturally
with our mouth full of nature.

Sifting the rush, we moor
disorder's specs of rhetoric
to advancements of speech
cohesive in their wave's
sand-flattened avalanche.

We inhabit the prattling
acting as tether to stretch
the further-fracturing start
that pronounced all its parts
an ageless all-together.

III

Along the shore the wind
rubs the outline
of a running man.
Erodes the inroads
his language gazed.
Opens a maze of space.
No sight but seeing
synchronizing total looks
with what all time will tell.

His legs track a set of prints
that lost their contents.
Having crammed imagination
into granular sensation, he leaves
the subreal to feeling's sculpture.
Micro-bits of collective drift
chiseling the truth of use.
This. Just this.
Just whet experience.

IV

The man is information after hydrogen.
His mind an expansive impasse
of complexity. Memory's plenum
making datum's destiny,
churning up enough undersea
to presage an end-kept course.
Tides in tension hasten
implications between out and in
safely dashing his indivisible run.

The ocean is as young as its occasion.
Pursuing what legs assume ages them.

Every wave is Wave merging
the meanings of wavering water.
Words vary to engage verse,
reversing to a useless thing.
Echoes backing out their beckoning
to resonate what creation
currently resumes again.
News convening One Event.
And this is it.

Forthcoming from Edition Muta

Survival Poem

we brained him with femur bones.
He tore our skull to the core.
We raged at the howling surrounding us.
Cooked food in a farther spot each day.
Our teeth canny as the unnamed.

This year we pray to cipher sutras
Computing the end of truthless use.
Appropriate the universe
from satellite dish to solar plexus
Crux our brains with a nugget of static.

Survival was once adrenalin and awe.
It saw no sun but shadow.
Now survival rivals all it knows.
Serums of ciphers expel cyanatic noise.
All ganglia is shared paraphernalia.

A circuit banters through synapse.
Births boastful vaults, but its shock
flops back to the iconic past.
Survival moans.
Telecasts its coma to outlast what lasts.

A LONG ROPE AT THE

EDGE OF THE VOID

Douglas Blazek

Each book by poet Douglas Blazek now being published by Edition Muta represents his life's work. However, it is not a mere reprinting of what was previously published in his 50-plus years of writing. Each, instead, is a complete revisioning accomplished through a 25-year process of re-writing, repeatedly, year after year, the original versions.

By mid-point in his writing life Blazek had published over 1000 poems, collected in over two dozen books and chapbooks, appearing in over 400 journals including *New Directions, American Poetry Review, Chicago Review, Poetry, TriQuarterly.* His editing a literary magazine *(Ole)* and publishing a small press *(Open Skull)* in the 1960's helped to free poetic restrictions and give impetus to the alternative publishing manifest in so much of today's poetry output.

Blazek is recognized as a primary instigator of the
Mimeo Revolution – a course correction for the culture,
dedicated to "making poetry dangerous". In this
endeavor he was instrumental in publishing formative
work by Charles Bukowski, d.a.levy and Robert Crumb
alongside other poets and artists central to the era.

Despite such prominence, Blazek describes the obligation
he felt to his poetic evolution as a *"self-lit fuse detonating
its own limits.*

*My poetry demanded to be fully realized, just as elements of nature
cannot be less than their inherent design. Knowing the futility of
achieving such perfection, if I were not to address what I had previously
published, the kinetic imagination of my early writing would merely
serve as an inferior prelude to a more successful later work that
advanced by observing its participation in the mirror of its creation.
In synthesizing those potentialties into their self-requested destiny, I
catalyzed a process that allowed a timeless dimension of ripeness
to exist in all my poetry.*

*Over the years, new poems were spliced into the manuscripts I was
rewriting. My poetics accelerated to sketch its dialectics on the synaptic
scrims of reality in a language of paradoxical correlation, suggestive, yet
simultaneously skin specific– unitary in consciousness. An inked cohe-
sion of mysterious signatures informed by an all-encompassing vision.
No old poem is old. Each is as fresh as if never breathed before, yet
preserves the bones its body first owned in its natality."*

The book now in your hands is neither representative
nor atypical of his other efforts. Neither chronologically
early nor late. Early and late are all in the same matrix,
all a portal to Blazek's life's work.

Edition Muta titles